I0605773

Weather Wonders

LEGENDARY LIGHTNING

Scott Wilken

Big Buddy Books

An Imprint of Abdo Publishing
abdobooks.com

abdobooks.com

Published by Abdo Publishing, a division of ABDO, PO Box 398166, Minneapolis, Minnesota 55439.

Printed in the United States of America, North Mankato, Minnesota
052025
092025

Design: Elena Klinkner, Mighty Media, Inc.
Production: Mighty Media, Inc.
Editor: Ruthie Van Oosbree
Cover Photograph: jerbarber/iStockphoto
Interior Photographs: Abestrobi/Wikimedia Commons, p. 23; arhip4/Shutterstock, pp. 6–7; Arturo_Pena_Romano_Medina/iStockphoto, p. 5; Asa Schlobohm/Shutterstock, p. 18; David W. Leindecker/Adobe Stock, pp. 22–23; Designua/Shutterstock, p. 11; dreamsquares/Adobe Stock, p. 28 (plate); Foloow/Adobe Stock, p. 14 (ball lightning); imageBROKER/Adobe Stock, p. 28 (brad); International Gemini Observatory/NOIRLab/NSF/AURA/A. Smith/Wikimedia Commons, pp. 16–17; ksena32/Adobe Stock, pp. 28 (wool); Lane V. Erickson/Shutterstock, p. 13; Matthew Dominick/Wikimedia Commons, pp. 26–27; mdesigner125/iStockphoto, pp. 20–21; Mighty Media, Inc., p. 29; Orion Media Group/Shutterstock, pp. 8–9; SkyroseStudio/Adobe Stock, p. 28 (pie pan); Tamas Kadar/DTU Space, Mount Visual/Daniel Schmelling, p. 25; Vitaly Zorkin/Adobe Stock, p. 28 (pencil); Wikimedia Commons, p. 14 (ball lightning engraving)
Design Elements: Mighty Media, Inc.

Library of Congress Control Number: 2024948565

Publisher's Cataloging-in-Publication Data
Names: Wilken, Scott, author.
Title: Legendary lightning / by Scott Wilken
Description: Minneapolis, Minnesota : Abdo Publishing, 2026 | Series: Weather wonders | Includes online resources and index.
Identifiers: ISBN 9781098296384 (lib. bdg.) | ISBN 9798384917816 (ebook)
Subjects: LCSH: Lightning--Juvenile literature. | Storms--Juvenile literature. | Weather--Juvenile literature. | Sky--Juvenile literature.
Classification: DDC 551.6--dc23

Contents

Electricity in the Sky

It's a stormy night. Suddenly there's a bright flash of light across the sky! It's a huge spark of electricity called lightning. Lightning can be very dangerous. But it can also look really amazing!

Most lightning bolts are about 2 to 3 miles (3.2 to 4.8 km) long.

Powerful Particles

Scientists believe lightning starts inside storm clouds. The **particles** in clouds move around and bump into one another. When they **collide**, each particle gains a **positive** or **negative** electrical **charge**. As the particles continue colliding, the electrical charges build up.

The particles in storm clouds are drops of water and tiny pieces of ice.

Opposites Attract

The **negative particles** in a cloud gather near the bottom. The ground and objects on the ground also have **charges**. Opposite charges are **attracted** to each other. So, the negative charges in the cloud and **positive** charges in objects or on the ground want to connect.

Lightning rods on buildings direct lightning safely to the ground.

A **negative current** of electricity shoots toward the ground. A **positive** current of electricity shoots up to meet it. When these currents join together, they create a long, **jagged** flash of light. This is a bolt of lightning!

LIGHTNING

Lightning also occurs between positive and negative charges within clouds (intra-cloud) and between separate clouds (cloud-to-cloud).

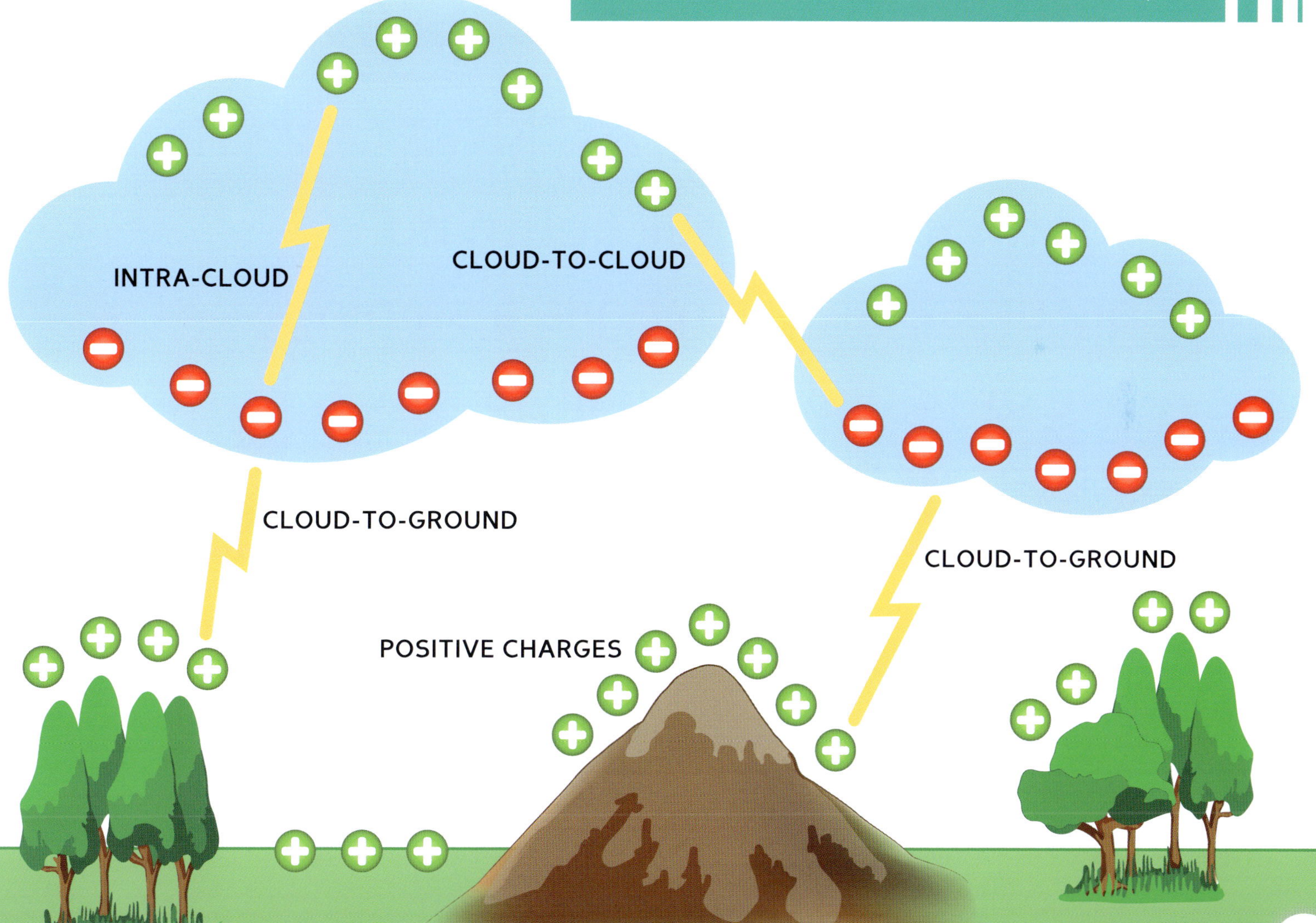

Ball Lightning

Sometimes a rare type of lightning called ball lightning occurs. Ball lightning is a shining ball of light. It is usually a few inches wide. A hissing sound and odor often come with it. Ball lightning usually forms close to the ground during thunderstorms.

People describe the color of ball lightning as white, red, orange, yellow, or blue.

People have reported seeing ball lightning drift along the ground and even into buildings!

There have been accounts of ball lightning sightings from all around the world since the 1100s. Some ancient stories about glowing balls may also have been based on ball lightning. But studying ball lightning is hard. It is rare and **unpredictable**. Scientists still don't know what causes it.

Transient Luminous Events

Most lightning occurs within storm clouds. However, several types of lightning occur above storm clouds. These are called transient luminous events (TLEs). TLEs include lightning sprites, elves, blue jets, and more. During strong thunderstorms, TLEs can put on amazing light shows!

Gigantic jets are another type of TLE.

TLEs such as lightning sprites are hard to study because they last for less than a second.

For hundreds of years, people have reported seeing flashes of light above thunderstorms. But no one knew what they were. In 1989, scientists in Minnesota took a **video** of a lightning sprite. This was the first TLE captured on camera. Scientists continue to try to learn more about them.

Lightning Sprites

Like most lightning, sprites are caused by electrical **charges** in storm clouds. However, instead of shooting toward the ground, sprites occur above clouds. Lightning sprites are red bursts of light. They can be about 30 miles (48 km) long.

Sometimes sprites have long lines below them called tendrils.

Elves

Elves were first observed by scientists in the 1990s. Like lightning sprites, elves are usually red. They are disk-shaped flashes of light caused by the electricity in a cloud. Elves start as small rings. Then they **expand** outward up to 300 miles (483 km) across.

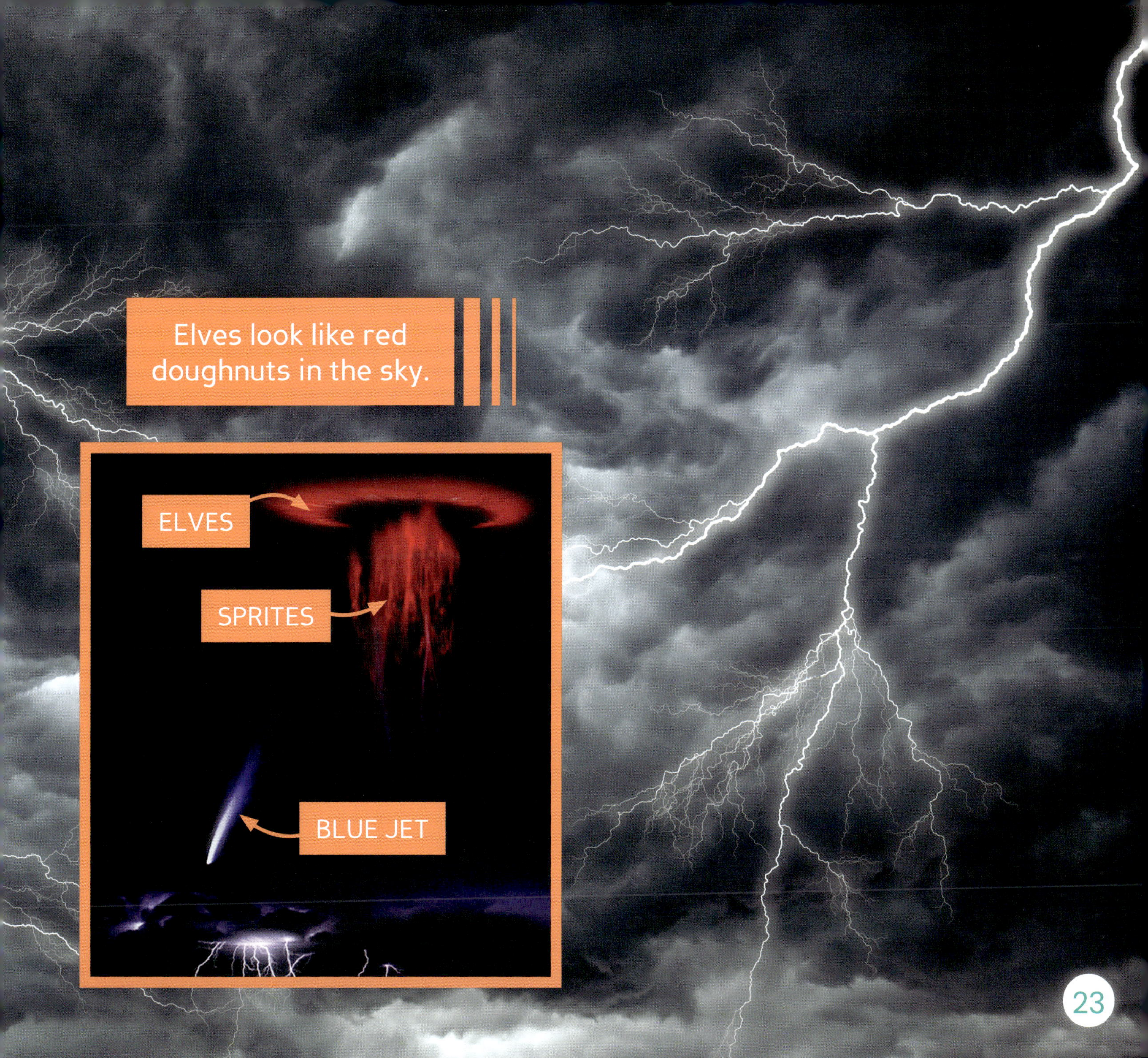
Elves look like red doughnuts in the sky.
ELVES
SPRITES
BLUE JET

Blue Jets

The existence of blue jets was confirmed in 1994 by scientists who flew around a thunderstorm in Arkansas. They saw a blue, cone-shaped flash of light above the clouds. This type of TLE became known as a blue jet.

Blue jets can be up to 35 miles (56.3 km) long.

Wondrous Weather

Strong thunderstorms can produce **spectacular** light shows. Weather wonders such as ball lightning and TLEs are exciting to see. But be sure to watch lightning from a safe place because it can also be dangerous!

Lightning is hot. It heats the air around it up to 50,000 degrees Fahrenheit (27,760°C).

Make a Mini Lightning Bolt!

What You Need

- brad
- aluminum pie pan
- pencil with eraser
- Styrofoam plate
- wool

What You Do

1. Poke the brad up through the middle of the pie pan.
2. Push the eraser end of the pencil onto the brad.
3. Turn the Styrofoam plate upside down. Quickly rub the bottom of the plate with the wool for a couple of minutes.

4. Use the pencil as a handle to pick up the pie pan. Set the pie pan on top of the upside-down plate.
5. Touch the pie pan with your finger. You should feel a shock. If you don't feel it, rub the bottom of the plate some more and place the pie pan back on top of it.
6. Once you feel the shock, try it again in a dark room. You should see a spark when you touch the pie pan!

Glossary

attract—to pull closer.

charge—an amount of electricity in an object. A charge can be either positive or negative.

collide—to come together with force.

current—the flow of electrically charged particles.

expand—to get bigger.

jagged—having a sharp, uneven, pointy shape.

negative—having the type of electrical charge carried by electrons, one of the particles in an atom.

particle—a very small piece of matter, such as an atom or molecule.

positive—having the type of electrical charge carried by protons, one of the particles in an atom.

spectacular—beautiful and amazing to look at.

unpredictable—behaving in ways that cannot be known in advance.

video—a moving-picture recording; a movie.

Online Resources

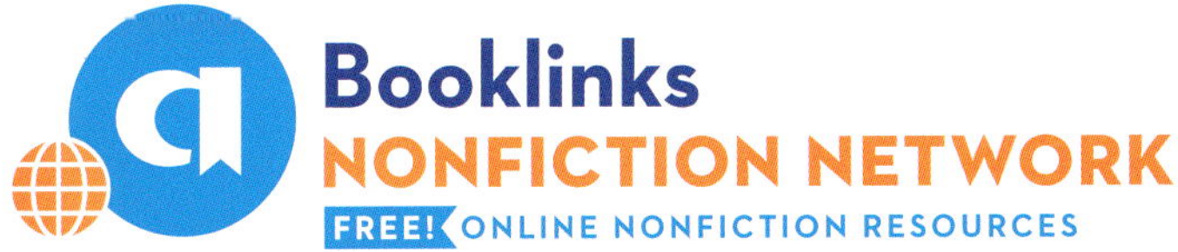

To learn more about lightning, please visit **abdobooklinks.com** or scan this QR code. These links are routinely monitored and updated to provide the most current information available.

Index